D1369992

Conflict
Resolution

The Practicing Administrator's Leadership Series
Jerry J. Herman and Janice L. Herman, Editors

**ROADMAPS
TO SUCCESS**

Other Titles in This Series Include:

The Path to School Leadership: A Portable Mentor
Lee G. Bolman and Terrence E. Deal

Holistic Quality: Managing, Restructuring, and Empowering Schools
Jerry J. Herman

Selecting, Managing, and Marketing Technologies
Jamieson A. McKenzie

Individuals With Disabilities: Implementing the Newest Laws
Patricia F. First and Joan L. Curcio

Violence in the Schools: How to Proactively Prevent and Defuse It
Joan L. Curcio and Patricia F. First

Women in Administration: Facilitators for Change
L. Nan Restine

Power Learning in the Classroom
Jamieson A. McKenzie

Computers: Literacy and Learning
A Primer for Administrators
George E. Marsh II

Restructuring Schools: Doing It Right
Mike M. Milstein

Reporting Child Abuse:
A Guide to Mandatory Requirements for School Personnel
Karen L. Michaelis

Handbook on Gangs in Schools:
Strategies to Reduce Gang-Related Activities
Shirley R. Lal, Dhyan Lal, and Charles M. Achilles

Conflict
Resolution
Building Bridges

Neil H. Katz
John W. Lawyer

CORWIN PRESS, INC.
A Sage Publications Company
Thousand Oaks, California

For information address:

Corwin Press, Inc.
A Sage Publications Company
2455 Teller Road
Newbury Park, California 91320

SAGE Publications Ltd.
6 Bonhill Street
London EC2A 4PU
United Kingdom

SAGE Publications India Pvt. Ltd.
M-32 Market
Greater Kailash I
New Delhi 110 048 India

Printed in the United States of America

Library of Congress Cataloging-in-Publication Data

Katz, Neil H.
    Conflict resolution: building bridges / Neil H. Katz, John W. Lawyer.
        p.   cm. — (Roadmaps to success)
    Includes bibliographical references (pp. 52-54) .
    ISBN 0–8039–6057–3
    1. School management and organization—United States. 2. School administrators—United States. 3. Conflict management—United States. 4. Educational leadership—United States. 5. Interpersonal relations—United States.   I. Lawyer, John W.   II. Title.
III. Series
LB2806.K276   1993
371.2'00973—dc20   93–6152

93 94 95 96   10 9 8 7 6 5 4 3 2 1

Corwin Press Production Editor: Marie Louise Penchoen

Contents

Foreword   vii
by Jerry J. Herman and Janice L. Herman

About the Authors   ix

Introduction   1

1   The Nature of Conflict   7
     • Sources of Conflict • Consequences of Conflict
     • Conflict Outcomes • Emotion in Conflict

2   Positive Attitudes Toward Conflict   20
     • Unconditional Positive Regard • Proactivity
     • Soft on People / Hard on the Problem
     • Unconditionally Constructive • Vision Driven
     and Outcome Oriented • Win/Win Frame of
     Reference • Openness and Respect for Diversity
     • Trust • Increased Autonomy • Growth and
     Development

3   A Conflict Resolution Model   27
     • Conflict Resolution Model • Stages

4   Conflict Resolution Process   37
        • Conflict Management • Negotiation

    Conclusion   51

    Annotated Bibliography and References   52

Foreword

This book is the first of three volumes on conflict resolution for school administrators. Each volume is useful as a stand-alone work; together, they provide school administrators with the essential attitude, knowledge, and skills to effectively resolve conflict in school settings.

The first volume, *Conflict Resolution: Building Bridges*, explores the nature of conflict and its principal sources, suggests helpful attitudes for framing conflict, and offers a useful model for conflict resolution and a process for effectively resolving conflict at an interpersonal or small group level. The model and process provide an effective conceptual framework for managing conflicts and negotiating solutions acceptable to the parties involved.

The second volume, *Resolving Conflict Successfully: Needed Knowledge and Skills*, presents the core skills essential for managing conflict and negotiating differences. These fundamental competencies include communication and rapport, reflective listening and pacing, and chunking and problem solving.

The third volume, *Managing Conflict in Schools*, focuses on processes for preventing conflict through effective human interaction. Four specific technologies are introduced that enable constructive human interaction: immediacy, agreement setting and management, mediation, and facilitation.

These works form a practical and comprehensive reference set for all educators who experience conflict situations in their schools or districts.

JERRY J. HERMAN
JANICE L. HERMAN
Series Co-Editors

About the Authors

Neil H. Katz is committed to self-actualization, nonviolence, and participative decision making as a way to influence change among individuals and in organizations and society. His primary interest is facilitating interactive learning and skill development about conflict and its resolution.

Katz serves in a leadership capacity in five different conflict resolution programs in the Maxwell School of Citizenship and Public Affairs at Syracuse University. He is the Director of the Program in Nonviolent Conflict and Change, Director of the Annual Summer Institute on Creative Conflict Resolution, Director of the University Conflict Resolution Consulting Group, Faculty Supervisor of the Campus Mediation Center, and Associate Director of the Program on the Analysis and Resolution of Conflicts.

Katz is a Danforth Teaching Fellow, a process consultant, a mediator, a facilitator, and a trainer in conflict resolution and negotiation skills. His clients include organizations in education, ministry, government, and education. Among his educational clients are the Danforth Foundation, the New York State Council of Superintendents, the New Jersey Department of Education, the U. S. National Science Foundation, the St. Louis Principal's Association, and numerous school systems in New York State and around the country.

Before receiving his doctorate and becoming a college professor, he taught junior high school.

Katz is the author or co-author of over 20 book chapters and articles on conflict resolution and nonviolence and coauthor (with Jack Lawyer) of three highly acclaimed workbooks, *Communication Skills for Ministry, Communication and Conflict Resolution Skills,* and *Communication and Conflict Management Skills.*

John W. Lawyer enjoys difference and change. He values himself as a choice maker and creator of processes and models that enable people to become lifelong learners. His primary interest is enabling others to build trusting environments, learn from their experience, and develop increasing autonomy in their professional and personal lives. In his work in facilitating change in organizations, Lawyer believes that creating dignity, meaning, and community in the workplace enables people to support and be committed to the idea behind their work. In this way work becomes satisfying, and both the organization as a whole and its members learn and develop.

In 1976 Lawyer founded Henneberry Hill Consultants, Inc., and currently serves as its president. It is an association of professional consultants dedicated to helping individuals, groups, and organizations improve their overall effectiveness in achieving their interests and goals. As a process consultant, he serves clients in education, business, government, social service, and church-related systems.

Prior to his entry into the consulting business, Lawyer managed an international business in which he pioneered the principle that leadership's primary task is to build trust, promote learning from experience, and enable people and work teams to achieve autonomy. These concepts were introduced in three of seven foreign manufacturing plants and one major domestic manufacturing plant.

Lawyer has a special interest in the development of models and skills for conflict management and interest-based negotiation. He has, in collaboration with others, published five books in the field of conflict resolution and change. He has been teaching three courses in Syracuse University's Annual Summer Institute on Creative Conflict Resolution since 1979.

Introduction

There is no doubt that an increasing amount of conflict is present in our society and especially in our schools. In recent years we have witnessed an alarming increase in physical fights, violence inflicted by weapons, violence against property, verbal harassment, and other forms of intimidating behavior that make many of our schools a threatening environment. Primary stakeholders in schools—students, teachers, administrators, board members, parents, and community members—are voicing their opinions more strongly and engaging in vigorous struggle in pursuit of their needs and beliefs. The ways in which people express their differences and attempt to get what they perceive they want or need greatly affects the learning environment. If disagreements are pursued by physical or verbal intimidation and coercion, schools will become increasingly tension-filled and frightening. In such a context, learning takes a secondary role to issues of personal safety. If, however, schools become model environments in which conflict and differences can be acknowledged and worked with creatively and nonviolently, the current situation can change. We need to create an educational delivery system in which knowledge acquisition is complemented by skill acquisition and attitude development. Interpersonal skills are especially needed to enable us to manage and resolve conflicts more effectively and efficiently in the interdependent world of today's schools.

Many different constituencies must work together in pursuit of the knowledge, skill, and attitude base that will ensure a safe, supportive environment conducive to student learning and enable students to become effective citizens in an increasingly complex society. This challenge must be taken up and led by our educational administrators. They are perceived as having the most authority in the school and are responsible for setting the tone for behavioral and attitudinal expectations. To accomplish the task of influencing school system leadership to adopt a more constructive approach to dealing with disputes and differences, administrators need sophisticated and effective conflict resolution skills to inspire themselves and others to create a positive environment of acceptance, mutuality, and autonomy.

In school systems and generally in society, conflict can emerge at a variety of human systems levels (Capelle, 1979). A school administrator can easily find himself/herself in a conflict situation in a number of possible human settings in any one day.

The diagram in Figure I.1 depicts a very simple community. This community consists of two school districts. The school districts have a main person in charge, the superintendent. There also is a building principal and a number of teachers. Let's look at this community from the point of view of one individual, Jim Law. Jim has several roles in the community. In the school system, Jim is a school principal in one of the two school districts. There are many potential conflicts that may be causing Jim concern. The first potential conflict is at the intrapersonal level. Jim might be recollecting a major difference with the school board and be experiencing considerable emotion around being treated disrespectfully. He is internally torn around what to do.

A second conflict may be occurring at the interpersonal level. Three possibilities include: (a) Jim and the district superintendent are not getting along well, (b) a conflict exists between Jim and one of the teachers around an emotional exchange that occurred when the teacher became defensive, and (c) an emotionally charged dispute has emerged between two teachers, and Jim is called in to mediate the conflict.

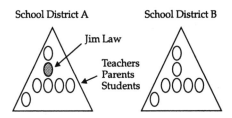

Figure I.1. A Hypothetical Community

The third potential conflict is at a group level. One possibility is that Jim Law is experiencing some problems with his fellow principals in the school district around which principal will fill a vacancy at one of the schools. Another conflict Jim could be involved in is with some of his teachers at school. Perhaps this group is not getting along well. There is some dissension, and some of the teachers don't like Jim. The conflict emerged in a group conversation about school improvement, and differences around cooperative learning strategies aroused strong emotion.

A fourth potential conflict is at an intergroup level. Two possibilities exist: (a) Jim is running a meeting between the fourth- and fifth-grade teachers, and one teacher blames the other for poor student performance. Emotions escalate, some teachers shout and others begin to cry. The fourth- and fifth-grade teachers each group together and stare at one another. (b) Jim's school is involved in antagonistic competition with school district B over the allocation of state funding for staff development.

Conflict might also exist at a fifth human systems level, the organization. A major racially charged incident occurred at a sports function in the school district. The faculty is split, and the school district makes the front page of the local newspaper.

At the sixth human systems level, Jim may be involved in an interorganizational conflict. Jim may be involved in a dysfunctional competition with a neighboring school district, or he may be involved in a dispute with the State Department of Education over the timing of certain deliverables with which the school is having trouble complying. Both Jim and the Commissioner get emotional.

Finally, at the seventh human systems level, Jim may be involved in community conflict. Jim attends a community meeting to discuss the budget, which calls for a significant tax increase. Emotions run strong at the public meeting. The whole community seems to be involved.

With this very simple example, we have hypothetically shown that it is possible for Jim Law to have conflicts at seven different human systems levels. These are: intrapersonal, interpersonal, group, intergroup, organizational, interorganizational, and community. Furthermore it is quite likely that the conflicts experienced at one level are somehow related to conflicts at other levels. For instance, Jim's conflict with the school board may be contributing to the conflict with the teachers; or, an interpersonal conflict with the superintendent may be contributing to the conflict between the fourth- and fifth-grade teachers; or, the conflict at an organizational level may have contributed to intrapersonal conflict.

The important learnings from this example are that conflicts occur at various human systems levels and that the various human systems levels are connected. The approach to dealing effectively with conflict varies with the level of the system involved. In this book, we will explore a broad conceptual understanding of conflict, explicate a useful generic model for resolving conflict regardless of the human systems level, and begin to develop the skills and attitudes required to manage the emotion involved in conflict situations and negotiate mutually acceptable solutions.

To understand conflict we need to situate it in a context of change. Conflict usually involves change in some way. A useful model for understanding the dynamics of change is indicated in "The Dynamics of Change Model" illustrated in Figure I.2.

Five concepts are illustrated in Figure I.2. The first, to the left, is the "Current Situation." The "Now Box" represents the current state; it exists in equilibrium, held there by forces pushing in both directions. Some forces are helping the system move toward the desired situation (the "Vision"), and some forces are hindering this movement. In the context of conflict, the "Now Box" represents both the current state of a conflict situation and its latent conflict potential at any human systems level.

The second area is the "Vision," the desired state of affairs. It represents the most desirable situation possible at a future time.

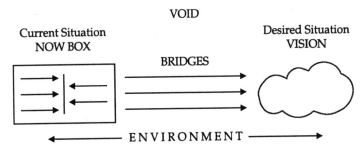

Figure I.2. The Dynamics of Change Model
Suzanne Baily, workshop notes, December 1990.

The "Vision" is resident in the imaginations of those in the human system, as well as those influenced by the human system or influencing the human system. In any human system a vision is the target. In the context of conflict, the "Vision" represents well-managed relationships. This means that when conflict emerges, the conflict is managed and the differences are negotiated to everyone's satisfaction.

The space between the "Now Box" and the "Vision" is the "Void." It includes the stakeholders and the situation in society and the world that influences both the current situation and the vision, as well as the guiding principles and norms of the society. It is a frightening, intimidating place typified by chaos. When conflict surfaces, those involved are pushed from the "Now Box" into the "Void" and experience this chaos. It is only by providing bridges that span from the "Now Box" to the "Vision" that the chaos of unmanaged conflict can be successfully navigated.

The fourth place in Figure I.2 is the "Environment," which supports both the "Now Box" and the "Vision". Any change in the environment will effect the "Now Box" in particular, often literally pushing people out of the "Now Box" into the "Void.". Whether the conflict itself or the environment causes the movement into the "Void," useful bridges are essential to move successfully from the "Now Box" to the "Vision".

The knowledge, attitudes, and skills offered in this book provide the bridges to successfully take charge of the process of getting from the "Now Box" to the "Vision" in conflict situations. These bridges will enable you to learn to manage conflict and negotiate differences in your personal and professional lives. The significant

Volume I: Conflict Resolution: Building Bridges
- Understanding the nature of conflict
- Positive attitudes toward conflict
- A conflict resolution model
- The conflict resolution process

Volume II: Resolving Conflict Successfully: Needed Knowledge and Skills
- Effective communication and rapport
- Listening and pacing for mutual understanding
- Chunking and problem solving for negotiation

Volume III: Managing Conflict in Schools
- *Immediacy*
- *Agreement setting and management* as conflict prevention
- *Mediation* for facilitating conflict resolution with others
- *Facilitation* for managing conflict in groups

Figure I.3. Bridges to Successful Conflict Resolution

bridges for our consideration are set forth in Figure I.3, "Bridges to Successful Conflict Resolution." In each of the three volumes on conflict resolutions, a chapter is allocated to each bridge.

These bridges incorporate critical knowledge, attitudes, and skills to enable school administrators to deal with conflict creatively and constructively.

In the first volume, Chapter 1 explores the nature of conflict and its sources. Looking at the sources of conflict provides a foundational understanding essential for grasping conflict resolution.

Chapter 2 suggests a positive attitudinal stance useful for those engaging in conflict resolution. The positive attitudes toward conflict, if adopted by conflict managers, greatly enhance their ability to achieve mutually satisfying outcomes in conflict situations.

Chapter 3 presents a model for understanding conflict resolution and the distinction between conflict management and negotiation. Understanding this distinction is essential to effectively using appropriate skills to resolve conflict.

Chapter 4 presents the specific processes for conflict management and negotiation. These protocols provide simple guidelines for resolving conflicts as they emerge at any human systems level.

The Nature of Conflict

Understanding the nature of something enables us to demystify a concept that might appear frightening without knowledge. In school settings particularly, conflict is often viewed negatively. This is largely due to the reality that conflict has traditionally been poorly managed from school board meetings to administrative staffs and in relationships among teachers, between teachers and students, and among students. This experience has connected the subject of conflict resolution to the pain of unresolved conflict, and we all naturally want to avoid pain. This chapter deals specifically with what conflict is, the sources of conflict, the consequences of conflict, conflict outcomes, and emotion in conflict.

Conflict is a situation or state between at least two interdependent parties, which is characterized by perceived differences that the parties evaluate as negative. This often results in negative emotional states and behaviors intended to overcome the opposition.

Conflict is an inevitable and all-pervasive element in our society and in the world. Although conflicts may end up in destruction and even death, conflicts may also result in increased effectiveness, enhanced relationships, and further goal attainment. Indeed, in human terms, conflict is one of the "engines of evolution" that allows us to learn, progress, and grow. Our goal is not to attempt to do away with conflict but rather to skillfully manage conflict to further its constructive potential (Katz and Lawyer, 1985).

The focus of this book is on conflict resolution—a communication process for managing a conflict and negotiating a solution. Managing the conflict involves creating constructive emotional states and enabling the disputing parties to understand their differences and similarities. Negotiation involves enabling the parties in the conflict to achieve a successful outcome with respect to their differences—an outcome that enables the parties to do better through jointly communicating and reaching an agreement than they could do without it.

Sources of Conflict

Conflict occurs within a context of perceived interdependence. An extreme example is a poker game, where the gains of one party are directly related to the losses of the other(s). If the parties in conflict were not interdependent—that is, if the actions of one party did not have some consequence for the other party—differences would exist, but conflict would not. This helps explain the fear of conflict. At best, conflict disrupts the order and established functioning of the group or personal relationship. However, if interdependence and a strengthened sense of community has value for everyone in the system and everyone perceives this value, then the interdependence can offer hope for a constructive resolution. In this situation, the interdependence is a force supporting the creation of some mutually acceptable solution for the conflict.

Conflict is a matter of perception. If none of the parties involved in an interaction perceives the situation to be one of incompatible outcomes, or if none of the parties perceives the situation to be problematic, then conflict does not exist. A situation of incompatible outcomes by itself is only a potential or latent conflict situation. For a conflict to move to an active stage, one or more of the parties must perceive the status quo as problematic and seek to alter the situation.

Conflict emerges from two primary sources: overt issues and covert issues. Covert issues are out-of-awareness psychological forces between individuals and within groups, especially between a group's leader and the group members.

Overt Conflict

In overt conflict, parties tend to perceive themselves as having incompatible outcomes. The word *outcome* in this context refers to what an individual wants; their preferred solution or position. Underlying these positions are interests—the reasons why an individual wants to achieve a specific outcome in the first place. Interests are an individual's perceptions and feelings about what is desirable or useful. Interests are central to an individual's behavior and are rooted in human needs and beliefs.

A need is a primary influencer of human behavior. When you experience a particular need, you are motivated to respond and take action. This motivated behavior is the result of the tension experienced when a need presents itself. The behavior is intended to satisfy the need.

A belief is a deeply felt priority that is freely chosen and, when acted on by an individual or group, is thought to improve the quality of life. A belief or conviction is therefore a choice that is viewed as positive by the individual making it.

A need then is a motivator and is tangible and concrete. A belief is a choice expressed in words and behavior and is intangible. Observing behavior by itself does not reveal whether it was motivated at the unconscious level by a need or a belief.

Interests can be based on needs or beliefs. They represent what causes you to choose, either consciously or unconsciously, a particular solution or pursue a particular desired outcome. Your position or outcome in a conflict is usually your initial best effort to find a solution to satisfy some underlying interests.

Conflicts of needs grow out of differences in the outcomes, personal goals, and aspirations of interdependent parties in the presence of scarce or undistributable resources. Two teachers desiring the same classroom might be experiencing a conflict of needs, as are educational organizations trying to reach the same market with their products or services.

Conflicts emerging around beliefs grow out of differences in convictions or perceptions about reality among interdependent parties. Ideological conflict falls into this category when contention is rooted in perceived differences in convictions or beliefs, accompanied by strong feelings. Your beliefs, for example, may favor one direction of movement over another. Then again, differences may lie not in direction but in the methods favored to reach the goal, when people have no interest other than defending their own belief system. To defend your own belief system without attacking another's is a difficult skill. For conflict resolution to occur all parties must focus on utilizing their differences in a quest for common ground and a shared outcome and real solutions.

Conflicts involving beliefs often underlie conflicts involving needs. Negotiation and problem solving are useful ways to resolve conflicts about needs. However, conflicts concerning beliefs cannot always be resolved. They must be managed even though no negotiated solution is available to the parties at a particular moment in time.

Covert Conflict

Covert conflict emerges in a relationship as a consequence of psychological projection. Psychological projection is the splitting off of unwanted emotions and behaviors, projecting them onto another, and investing the other with those emotions or behaviors.

Consequences of Conflict

Conflict per se is neutral—neither good nor bad. It can have positive as well as negative consequences for the parties involved and for the larger social system of which the disputing parties are members.

Positive Results of Conflict

On the positive side, conflict can provide an opportunity for creativity, renewed energy, drama, development, and growth to individuals, groups, and organizations, resulting in increased cohesion and trust. It can lead, as well, to more effective personal and organizational performance.

Positive consequences for individuals involved in conflict can include:

1. *Reconciliation of the interests of the disputing parties:* Most conflicts can end with at least some satisfaction of the legitimate interests of the parties involved, usually through working out an integrative agreement of mutual benefit. Rarely do conflicts have to end in clear-cut win/lose outcomes.

2. *A sharpened sense of identity and solidarity:* As individuals engage in conflict, their sense of who they are as persons with unique needs tends to be sharpened. As they differentiate themselves from one another, they uncover ways in which they are similar and different. The similarities enhance rapport and a sense of solidarity; the differences help to sharpen a sense of identity and unique contribution to the whole.

3. *Interaction:* Conflict tends to promote interaction at an interpersonal level and create a new system of which all parties are instantly a part. As one party changes, all the other parties must then change to restore the equilibrium.

4. *Internal change:* As disputing parties experience conflict and engage in dialogue with others of differing needs and beliefs, they are confronted with the prospect of making adjustments in their positions. The pressure to explore new ideas and feelings can challenge an individual to move from rigidity to flexibility, with consequent internal change.

5. *Clarifying the real problem:* Conflicts often emerge around different solutions to a particular problem shared by the disputing parties. As dialogue is conducted and the parties begin to explore the interests underlying the contrary positions, the real problem can be identified and addressed.

Conflicts often involve groups and occur between group members. Conflict can have positive consequences for all group members that are parties to the dispute. Some of them include:

1. *Increased trust:* As individuals enter into any experience with one another in group settings, trust is low, resulting in defending behaviors on the part of groups members. In conflict situations this tendency is exacerbated, because the disputing parties perceive the possibility of their failing and being hurt. As individuals share their thoughts and feelings with one another in the group, trust builds, freeing energy previously spent in defending.

2. *Increased productivity and results:* As conflict is exposed and the parties involved express their thoughts and feelings, the group can be healed of some of the negative feelings that tend to prevail in conflict situations. As the group is freed of diverting emotions and discovers new solutions, its productivity and creativity can increase.

3. *Group unity:* Conflict fosters a sense of group unity and identity as disputing parties reconcile individual differences. Without differences and diversity, groups can become stagnant and lose a sense of its creativity and uniqueness.

Negative Results of Conflict

Often the positive benefits of conflict are overshadowed by harmful consequences that result when disputing parties attempt to achieve their goals at the expense of others. Such forcing exchanges often bring about an escalation of the conflict that is difficult to reverse. When forcing methods are used, any of the following negative consequences can follow:

1. Minor differences can escalate into major conflicts involving actions imposed by a power person or group on another, resulting in greater loss to the system as a whole.

2. The number of issues in the conflict can increase, resulting in greater complexity and greater difficulty in managing the situation.

3. Specifics can give way to global concerns, which often cause the person to be equated with and confused with the issue at stake, or the entire relationship between the disputing parties can be called into question.

4. The intention can shift from getting a specific interest satisfied to beating the other parties at all costs.

5. The number of parties can increase, making it even more difficult to deescalate the conflict (Pruitt and Rubin, 1986, p. 7).

✳ Conflict Outcomes

Conflict always manifests itself in terms of some specific outcomes. Three possible outcomes can emerge:

1. Dominance or imposition, resulting in resentment and sometimes destructive consequences.

2. Withdrawal or avoidance, resulting in resentment and lowered self-image.

3. Compromise or resolution, resulting in at least some beneficial consequences being achieved (Kriesberg, 1982, pp. 291-299).

These outcomes are dependent on the approach or strategy used to deal with the conflict. The choice among alternative strategies can spell the difference between resentment and mutual respect. In summary, these outcomes result from five basic approaches, or strategies, available to address the conflict situation:

- *Collaboration:* A win/win strategy based on a clear positive vision and the use of problem solving to ensure that the interests of all parties are met. This approach results in maintaining strong interpersonal or intergroup relationships while ensuring that all parties achieve their interest.
- *Compromise:* A mini-win/mini-lose strategy based on a solution that partially satisfies the interests of the parties involved. This approach results in the parties' attempting to win as much as possible while preserving the interpersonal or intergroup relationships as much as possible.
- *Accommodation:* A yield-lose/win strategy wherein one party yields to the other party (or parties) to protect and preserve the relationships involved.

- *Controlling:* A win/lose strategy based on imposing a particular preferred solution on the other party (or parties). This
  approach results in sacrificing the interpersonal or intergroup relationship to achieve a desired outcome, regardless
  of the consequences to the other party or parties.
- *Avoiding:* A lose/lose strategy based on withdrawing and
  choosing to leave the conflict. This approach results in aban-
  doning both the desired outcome and the opportunity to
  enhance the relationship.

These alternative strategies for attending to disputes and differences suggest a two-dimensional model for conflict based on how
an individual or group balances concern about the positions and
concern about the relationships involved in the conflict situation.
There are people who shrink away at the first signs of conflict,
whereas others typically confront the conflict and seek a solution
in which the outcomes of all parties will be met. Some people are
so concerned about the possibility of damaging their relationships
with the other party (or parties) that they concede their positions
practically at the first sign of a conflict. Others attempt the "half-a-
loaf" tactic, trying to achieve as much of their positions as possible
while doing as little damage to the relationship as possible. Still
others are so concerned with achieving their positions that they
damage or destroy the relationship with the other party (or parties).

Your fundamental approach to conflict is a choice you make that
achieves a balance between concern for the relationships and for
the desired positions of the parties involved in a particular situation. The five strategies, or approaches, to conflict are shown in
"The Two-Dimensional Model of Conflict" in Figure 1.1. The conflict strategies, or approaches, differ in the degree of emphasis the
conflicting parties place on their relationship and their desired
positions.

The win/win approach to conflict management is one in which
the problem is viewed as external to the persons involved. The opposing parties collaborate to seek a high-quality solution that
meets their mutual needs while preserving their relationship. The
win/win strategy involves the use of problem-solving methods
and is generally the ideal approach for managing both conflicts of
needs and conflicts of beliefs, because it resolves the conflict and

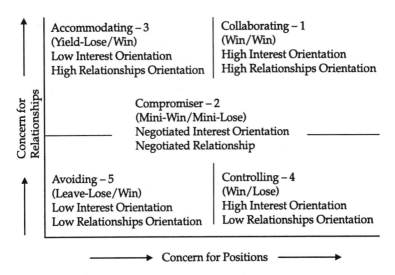

Figure 1.1. The Two-Dimensional Model of Conflict

results in mutual respect between the conflicting parties. This approach or strategy usually enables all parties to a conflict to do better than they might do without the ideas and actions of the other parties.

The other strategies for conflict management—which, as a group, might be thought of as forcing strategies or approaches—are those in which each party tackles the problem separately, with the problem coming between the parties and distancing them, and with one or both parties ending up settling for a solution that does not meet their interests. The forcing approaches generally represent less-than-optimal methods for managing conflicts, because they result in some resentment and continue to distance the disputing parties from one another.

In making choices about your approach to conflict and noticing the approaches used by others, remember that:

- People make choices about their approach to conflict for reasons that make sense to them.
- No one approach is better than another in every situation.
- People change their approach in order to adapt to the demands of new situations.

The approach to conflict you choose is contingent on the circumstances of the particular situation. Different situations call for different approaches. Some specific applications that call for each of these approaches are grouped by strategy as follows, starting with the most preferred approach and ending with the least preferred:

Collaboration

- When concerns are too important for compromise.
- When no party has a good solution and merging insights offer creative possibilities.
- When complete resolutions are needed without leftover negative feelings.

Compromise

- When the goal or outcome of the conflict is not worth the time and energy required for collaboration.
- When a quick and temporary expedient settlement is acceptable.
- When collaboration doesn't work out and the conflict cannot otherwise be resolved.

Accommodation

- When one party has a decidedly better solution (position).
- When the issues involved are considerably more important to one party.
- When continued competition could damage the relationship, lead to escalated conflict in the future, or lead to a loss of the relationship.

Controlling

- When quick, decisive action is vital.
- When an issue is important and an unpopular course of action needs implementation.
- When an issue is vital to the long-term success of an organization.

Avoiding

- When an issue is trivial in relation to other more pressing concerns.

- When there is no possibility of either settling or resolving the issue.
- When one of the parties has low power in relation to the other.
- When the potential damage of confrontation outweighs the benefits of resolution.

As you become increasingly skilled, you will find yourself choosing the collaborative strategy because it inherently satisfies both the substantive interest behind your position as well as maintaining and enhancing your relationships.

✖ Emotion in Conflict

Emotion is present in any conflict. Most often this emotion is perceived by the parties as negative and expressed both verbally and nonverbally. Emotion can be thought of as energy. In any relationship, there is an underlying level of emotional energy that is based on perception of resentment or mutual respect. In a relationship characterized by resentment, or other destructive emotional states, the parties are predisposed to engage in conflict. The feelings that occur tend to be intense. Resentment can be thought of as unexpressed conflict, which causes feelings of mistrust and distances the parties involved from one another. Such negative feelings often result from:

- Use of inappropriate conflict management strategies
- Anticipation of future clashes
- Outward behavior that causes tension
- Unsettled grievances that have accumulated over time
- Power building by one or both parties
- Stereotyping by one or both parties

In a relationship characterized by underlying mutual respect, negative feelings are usually expressed openly, the conflict is engaged from a positive frame of reference, and it is brought to a mutually satisfying conclusion. Such a situation is characterized by:

- Use of a collaborative conflict-management strategy as soon as a conflict is recognized
- Open expression of thoughts and feelings
- Anticipation of the other party's interests
- Acknowledgement and appreciation of the other party's positive behavior
- Respect for diversity and individual differences

Figure 1.2 illustrates part of a conflict cycle, consisting of two episodes of conflict. As shown in the graph, the level of emotional energy in the relationship and the degree of residual conflict are at first moderately high, indicating a moderate level of resentment. The emergence of open conflict in each episode begins with a "triggering event"—a precipitating occurrence that shifts the balance of power or changes a situation. The conflict situations themselves are overt expressions of perceived incompatible differences, involving specific instances of infringement, high energy, and expressed strong feelings. The significant difference between the two episodes lies in how they are managed.

The first conflict episode is handled using a forcing approach, which suppresses the open conflict but results in a considerably higher level of emotional energy than existed at first. In this instance a higher level of underlying resentment in the relationship results. The relationship is therefore even riper for a subsequent episode of conflict, which promptly breaks out following another triggering event.

The second conflict episode, in contrast, is handled using a win/win problem-solving approach, which results in lowering the level of negative emotional energy in the relationship. This increases the level of mutual respect and builds a more trusting relationship. The use of this win/win approach, then, results in working out the overt manifestations of the conflict and alters the nature of the relationship itself. Future conflicts are less likely to occur, and those conflicts that do occur are less likely to be intense.

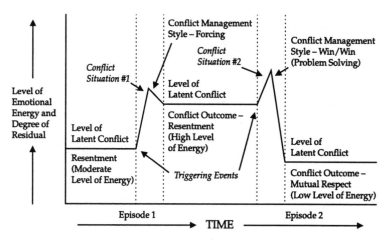

Figure 1.2. Conflict Cycle

2

Positive Attitudes Toward Conflict

WHOLE CHAPTER

The future of schools will, for the most part, be determined by leaders at the local site level. The creativity and imagination of administrators, teachers, board members, parents, and community members will establish the vision and the direction for our schools.

How we frame things significantly affects our behavior and the influence we have on others. A frame is the context through which we view something, as well as the process we use to select, delete, and arrange what we are talking about. It refers to how we assign meaning and make sense out of something. A frame can be thought of as a mental pattern or map or template that promotes our understanding.

An attitude is a frame we use to sharpen our understanding of the world. Attitudes act as filters through which we process our experience of the world. Attitudes shape our perceptions and affect the internal representations we make of our experience, the feelings we have about that experience, and the physiology we adapt in response to those perceptions.

Attitudes become self-fulfilling prophesies. If an administrator sees children as untrustworthy, he or she will act toward them as not being worthy of trust. With this view the administrator is likely to implement policies of high control with students and promote their dependency rather than autonomy.

1. Unconditional positive regard of others involved in a conflict
2. Proactivity, one of taking initiative and making things happen
3. Being soft on people and hard on the problem
4. Being unconditionally constructive in a conflict situation
5. Being vision driven and outcome oriented
6. A win/win frame of reference
7. Openness, respect, and appreciation for diversity
8. Trust as the primary foundation of relationships
9. Learning from experience as a key to increasing autonomy
10. Viewing conflict as an opportunity for personal growth and development

Figure 2.1. Ten Attitudes for the Successful Resolution of Conflict

The effort to reform schools will require knowledge, skill, and attitudes that create dignity, meaning, and community throughout the school environment. Positive attitudes are especially critical.

Stephen Covey in his book *The Seven Habits of Highly Successful People* (Covey, 1989) illustrates the essential importance of fundamental attitudes toward achieving success in any endeavor. Covey appropriately points out the connected nature of knowledge, skills, and attitudes, and the importance of each of these in forming a successful person.

Positive attitudes toward conflict, complimented by congruent knowledge and skills, are critical to the successful management and resolution of conflict. We have identified ten attitudes that, if adopted, will lay a foundation for the successful management of conflict and the negotiation of differences, and ensure that the interests of the conflicting parties are met. These ten attitudes are illustrated in Figure 2.1.

Each of the ten attitudes is elaborated in the following sections.

Unconditional Positive Regard

This attitude flows from the universal principle that invites everyone to "love one another"—a core principle of all the great religions. We are not so naive as to think that loving others is a practical consideration in society today but that it *is* a useful way to be. In a sense we are asking that you "act as if" you feel unconditionally positive toward the other party(s) in a conflict situation.

As an administrator you might not like a teacher, such as when you are in the same room and find him or her particularly aggravating. You find other teachers more compatible, seem to share common interests with them, and feel they believe the same things about the world that you do. When the aggravating situation with the teacher is emotionally charged, and is not behaviorally based, it is likely a relationship in which projection and some transference is present. This phenomenon is present among all groups of people and the source of many conflicts in our society.

We need to recognize the possibility of projection and transference and systematically base our relationships with others on a foundation of trust and on their specific behavior in situations that involve us. This is especially useful because, in our view, people are fundamentally positively intentioned; that is, their behavior makes sense to them given the way they see, hear, and feel the world and is based on a set of expectations that their actions will have positive outcomes. Acting "as if" this is true can have a profound affect on your ability to successfully manage conflict and negotiate win/win solutions to human differences.

Proactivity

An attitude of proactivity is critical to success in conflict resolution. A proactive person is positively motivated to "move toward" dealing with conflict constructively and creatively when it arises. The proactive person views conflicts and the conflict resolution process as opportunities for growth and change rather than as a necessity to maintain relationships. The proactive person would recognize a conflict situation readily and initiate a conflict management process to make something useful happen, rather than wait and react only to another's initiative. The person who chooses to be proactive can have a profound influence in bringing about win/win solutions to disputes and differences.

Soft on People / Hard on the Problem

In conflict resolution it is helpful to separate the people from the problems that are in contention. It is useful to perceive people as "resources" that will help you deal with the problem at hand. With more resources working on the same problem, more creative options to meet the mutual interests are likely to surface. When you act with this attitude, you are using your energy to attack the problem without attacking the people. According to Roger Fisher and William Ury, a useful rule of thumb is to give positive support to the human beings on the other side equal in strength to the vigor with which you emphasize the problems (Fisher and Ury, 1983).

Unconditionally Constructive

In conflict situations an attitude of being totally and unconditionally constructive is not only useful but essential. This means that regardless of what others do, you are to act as if they are positively intentioned at some level.

You need to expect that others might act in ways to get their needs met at your expense. Even in situations in which others use unscrupulous techniques, it is useful to adopt an attitude of constructiveness throughout the conflict resolution process. This means simply acting "as if" the others in the dispute or difference will be constructive. This attitude in itself is infectious and assists the process of gaining a win/win solution to the conflict.

Vision Driven and Outcome Oriented

When you find yourself in a conflict, it is important to have a vision of how you would like to behave and be perceived and what you would like to accomplish by your involvement in the situation. Your vision might include your view of what you would like the relationships to be after the conflict is dealt with and how you would like to be remembered. What specific outcomes are you pursuing for yourself and your constituents in both the short term and long term? Is your vision of yourself as a conflict manager congruent with the specific means you are using and the specific outcomes you are pursuing in this particular conflict? A conflict strategy that is in sync with your specific outcomes and general vision will provide more satisfactory results.

Win/Win Frame of Reference

It is important to approach a conflict resolution with the belief that an outcome that serves mutual interests is desirable and possible. This belief will allow you to access the appropriate skills for a collaborative strategy and to remain unconditionally constructive even when the other conflict parties are engaging in destructive acts. To proceed with a win/win attitude, it is helpful to think of the other parties as "conflict partners" rather than "conflict adversaries" (Weeks, 1992). This change in language will be helpful in maintaining the focus and discipline necessary to be successful in the win-win paradigm.

Openness and Respect for Diversity

Openness implies a willingness to express your thoughts and feelings. Conflict resolution experts need to have a healthy and open attitude toward diverse viewpoints and people from various backgrounds who might see, hear, and feel the world in different ways than they do. It is useful to view this diversity as an added incentive to be involved in the rich tapestry of life and human experience. Then, diverse thoughts, feelings, ideas, and styles will be respected and appreciated for the new information they add to the understanding of the problem, as well as options for possible solutions.

Trust

Trust is the foundation of all quality human relationships. Trust implies being trustworthy at the personal level and trusting at the interpersonal level. Trustworthiness involves both character and competence. As an administrator, you would tend to trust a teacher if the teacher was competent and possessed good character. Lacking either would tend to erode your trust.

Character involves integrity, maturity, and an abundance mentality. A person acts with integrity who is congruent, who makes clear agreements and sticks to them, and whose life habits live out what he or she values. Maturity implies that a person has courage balanced with consideration—an ability to act with prudence and judgment, taking the interests of others into consideration. An abundance mentality implies the ability to move beyond the apparent limits of a situation. Viewing a conflict as dividing up a fixed pie is more limiting than viewing the situation as an expandable pie. Trusting another involves believing that the other will act toward you with character and competence (Covey, 1989).

The ability to be trustworthy and to trust is essential to building human relationships. Rapport and high-quality relationships promote the effective management of conflict.

Increased Autonomy

Once trust is established, learning becomes possible. Learning from our experience provides the foundation for achieving autonomy. Autonomy is a state achieved by an individual or group in which either is self-governing. Autonomy is typified by the ability to be self-descriptive, self-regulating, self-evaluating, and self-correcting. An individual or group that is autonomous can be said to be self-directing. The autonomous state is characterized by five resource states, as follows:

- *Consciousness:* The ability to sense with awareness what is happening in the world with a sharpened sense of acuity.
- *Precision:* The ability to think, speak, and act with precision.
- *Flexibility:* The ability to readily shift to another, and more effective, course of action when stuck.
- *Community:* The ability to take the needs and interests of the group and the community as a whole into consideration.
- *Efficacy:* The ability to know that what you do makes a difference in the world.

As an administrator, it is useful to be open to increased autonomy in yourself, as well as to promote increased autonomy in the individuals and groups operating within your school system.

An openness to increased autonomy, the ability to direct and shape our own lives, is a helpful attitude consistent with the knowledge and skills presented in this book. The conflict resolution model developed is an empowering strategy which assists those involved in conflict resolution to more completely understand their interests and the interests of others, and engage a problem-solving process to identify and act on options to satisfy those interests. The model emphasizes the right and ability to make choices for oneself freely, after considering the alternatives and possible consequences. Other skills promoted in the book enable us to remain resourceful, a state defined by Laborde (1988) as your optimal emotional and physical condition, in which the resources you have gathered during your life are readily available to you.

Growth and Development

In conflict situations you are bombarded with a range of ideas, opinions, and feelings which necessitate an exploration of who we are, what we believe, what we want, and how we are willing to pursue what we want. Every conflict situation is an opportunity for self-examination and personal growth about ourselves and human behavior in general. In addition, if the conflict is within or between organizations, we can learn enormous amounts of useful information about our group and organization. Conflict provides the momentum to change and grow developmentally and to more fully realize our human potential as individuals and groups.

A Conflict Resolution Model

Conflict resolution is a communication process for managing a conflict and negotiating a solution. It is best understood using a working model with two key elements—conflict management and negotiation.

Conflict management is a communication process for changing the destructive emotional states in a conflict to constructive emotional states that allow working out a joint solution to the conflict. Negotiation is a communication process for enabling disputing parties to achieve a mutually agreed-on outcome with respect to their differences.

The win/win or collaborative strategy in conflict requires a special approach to negotiation: interest-based negotiation. Interest-based negotiation is a communication process for developing an integrative agreement that meets the interests of the differing parties.

Resolving conflicts to achieve positive outcomes involves two distinct elements, as shown in Figure 3.1. The first element, *conflict management,* deals with the attitudes and strong negative emotions usually associated with a conflict situation. It involves defusing the accompanying emotional energy and achieving a mutual understanding of similarities and differences. The conflict management is complete when destructive behavior has been reduced and hostile attitudes lessened. However, the causes of the conflict still

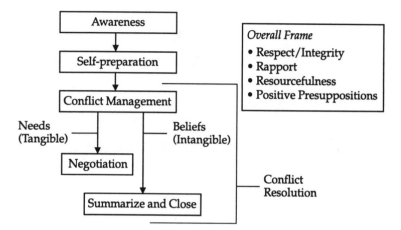

Figure 3.1. Conflict Resolution—Working Model

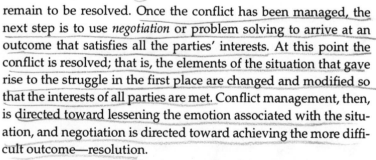

remain to be resolved. Once the conflict has been managed, the next step is to use *negotiation* or problem solving to arrive at an outcome that satisfies all the parties' interests. At this point the conflict is resolved; that is, the elements of the situation that gave rise to the struggle in the first place are changed and modified so that the interests of all parties are met. Conflict management, then, is directed toward lessening the emotion associated with the situation, and negotiation is directed toward achieving the more difficult outcome—resolution.

The material in the following sections of this chapter describe a sequence of actions that are useful in managing and resolving conflicts. We have organized these suggested actions in terms of a model. The model proposes the order in which the skills should be used. The model provides a framework for deciding what actions to take at what time and a desired outcome for each action to be taken during the conflict. It describes what you should do, why you should do it, and when you should do it.

Conflict Resolution Model

The conflict resolution working model involves an overall frame and four stages. The four stages are awareness, self-preparation, conflict management, and negotiation. These stages are predicated on the following principles:

- The essence of conflict is the high emotional energy around perceived differences.
- The essence of conflict management is the defusing or lessening of the high emotional energy and the mutual understanding of differences.
- Resolution of the conflict often involves negotiation (problem solving) to bring about an outcome that is mutually satisfying.
- The keys to effective conflict resolution are the ability to:
  - Reflectively listen to ensure understanding.
  - Maintain rapport at all times.
  - Differentiate positions from interests.
  - Work toward mutual resolution through dovetailing of interests.

An elaborated version of the conflict resolution model is shown in Figure 3.2. A description of the overall frame and the stages of the model is contained in the following sections:

Overall Frame

A presupposition in this interest-based conflict management working model is an overall frame for conflict resolution that is positive. This frame includes:

- Respect and integrity
- Rapport
- Resourcefulness
- A constructive attitude

Respect and Integrity

Respect means that you view every person with positive regard regardless of the behavior evidenced by the person. You may deplore the behavior and find it totally unacceptable. You refuse, however, to allow that behavior to contaminate your regard of the others in the conflict as human persons deserving your respect.

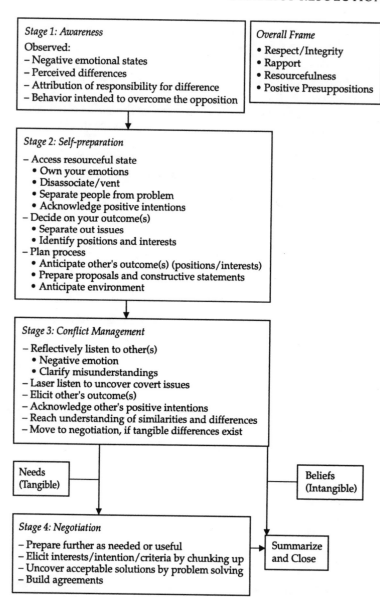

Stage 1: Awareness
Observed:
– Negative emotional states
– Perceived differences
– Attribution of responsibility for difference
– Behavior intended to overcome the opposition

Overall Frame
• Respect/Integrity
• Rapport
• Resourcefulness
• Positive Presuppositions

Stage 2: Self-preparation
– Access resourceful state
  • Own your emotions
  • Disassociate/vent
  • Separate people from problem
  • Acknowledge positive intentions
– Decide on your outcome(s)
  • Separate out issues
  • Identify positions and interests
– Plan process
  • Anticipate other's outcome(s) (positions/interests)
  • Prepare proposals and constructive statements
  • Anticipate environment

Stage 3: Conflict Management
– Reflectively listen to other(s)
  • Negative emotion
  • Clarify misunderstandings
– Laser listen to uncover covert issues
– Elicit other's outcome(s)
– Acknowledge other's positive intentions
– Reach understanding of similarities and differences
– Move to negotiation, if tangible differences exist

Needs
(Tangible)

Beliefs
(Intangible)

Stage 4: Negotiation
– Prepare further as needed or useful
– Elicit interests/intention/criteria by chunking up
– Uncover acceptable solutions by problem solving
– Build agreements

Summarize
and Close

Figure 3.2. Conflict Resolution—Working Model (Elaborated Version)

You also act with integrity in conflict situations; that is, you are honest and open in all your dealings with the person to the extent that the situation allows. Your fundamental perspective is to seek solutions that are mutually beneficial. You, therefore, avoid getting your needs met at the expense of the other person.

Rapport

Essential to the effective management of conflict is rapport: the ability to create a relationship of responsiveness and attentiveness with the other. In conflict situations you need to be able to gain rapport and maintain it throughout the conflict resolution process.

Resourcefulness

To be resourceful is to be able to maintain a state of attentiveness, focus, and the ability to access effective skills. A state of resourcefulness is typified by a mental alertness and a relaxed demeanor that allows you to function effectively even in stressful situations.

Positive Presuppositions

This approach to conflict and our conflict resolution working model is based on the following positive presuppositions (these presuppositions may or may not actually be always correct but are useful to accept in conflict situations and act "as if" they are true):

- People have the resources to make the changes they wish to make.
- People are doing the best they can at any particular moment in time.
- A mutually acceptable solution is available and is desirable (that is, shared interests).
- Cooperation is preferable to competition.
- The views openly expressed by others are perceived by them to be legitimate representations of their true positions.
- The existence of differing opinions is helpful.
- The disputing parties are capable of competing but will choose to cooperate as a consequence of the intervention.

Stages

The conflict resolution model involves four stages:

Stage 1: Awareness

This is the first stage in the conflict resolution model. It involves coming to awareness of the negative emotional states in a conflict. It emerges around the awareness of perceived differences, usually because of:

- An assertion, where one party attempts to influence another party or parties to achieve his or her needs.
- One party takes a stand on an issue that is opposed by another party or parties.
- One party attempts to exercise power or control over the actions or behavior of the other party or parties.
- Feedback, where one party gives feedback to another and the feedback is resisted.
- Imposed sanctions, where one party intentionally harms the other to get his or her needs met.

Stage 2: Self-preparation

The second stage of the conflict resolution model involves accessing a resourceful state, deciding on your outcome, and planning the steps to achieve it. This stage can take place quickly or can involve a considerable amount of time, depending on the context.

Accessing and Maintaining a Resourceful State

The most critical step in this stage involves accessing and maintaining a resourceful state. You will first need to "own" and take charge of your own emotions or internal states. A belief tends to exist that emotional states just occur or are somehow controlled by other's actions or behaviors. We believe that emotional states are chosen by people at some level and are controllable. Owning and controlling your emotional state and then ensuring that you can maintain a resourceful state throughout a conflict situation is essential in successfully resolving conflicts.

In conflict situations it is useful to separate the people from the problem or issue. A reality in dealing with conflicts is that you are dealing with human beings who have emotions, deeply held beliefs, and different personal histories. Building a relationship of trust, understanding, and respect is essential to having conflicts managed well and outcomes negotiated successfully.

In reality two kinds of interests exist in a dispute: the content or substance and the relationship. Failing to deal with the relationship with sensitivity can be disastrous. The challenge is to separate the substance from the relationship and place the relationship first.

Dealing with the relationship first means obtaining and maintaining rapport throughout the conflict resolution process. The key is to separate the people from the problem and deal with people as human beings and with the problem or issue on its merits.

Deciding on Your Outcome

In some instances you might have the time to decide your outcome and plan the process before the conflict is managed. In other situations, you might find yourself well into a conversation and will need to manage the conflict and prepare as best you can during the process. Should you have the time, determining your outcome and planning the process is advantageous.

An outcome is what you want to achieve in a particular situation. A particular outcome in a negotiation context is often referred to as a position.

Distinguishing between position and interests is essential for effective conflict management. Roger Fisher and William Ury make the distinction clearly in their work *Getting to Yes* (1983), as follows:

- *Position:* What you decide you want in a dispute or difference—a particular solution that is predetermined.
- *Interest:* What caused you to decide—your specific needs in the dispute or difference that prompted you to take a particular position or arrive at a particular solution.

Your position is essentially a specific solution that will achieve your outcome. Underlying your position are your interests. It is your interests, your fundamental needs in a situation, that usually motivate you to arrive at a particular solution. For example, two people at the library are reading in the same room. One wants the window open, and the other wants it closed. The initial positions and underlying interests are illustrated in Figure 3.3. Once the underlying interests that motivate the positions (that is, fresh circulating air and avoiding the draft) are uncovered, a win-win solution that meets both parties interests is possible (open window in the next room).

Conflicts of needs are usually around positions. When people "lock into" positions, the best outcome that can be hoped for is a compromise. The possibility of achieving a collaborative solution in a dispute or difference emerges because of the commonality of the interests of the parties. This commonality allows for integrating the interests to achieve a resolution to the conflict that is satisfying and pleasing to all parties involved.

Knowing what your outcome or particular solution is and the interests that underlie it will help you enormously in managing conflict and negotiating mutually acceptable resolutions. An outcome exists for each issue in the conflict. Often more than one issue is present. Your outcomes and the interests that underlie them need to be identified for each issue.

Planning the Process

After deciding on your outcomes, further anticipation of the conflict episode is useful. Anticipate and prepare for the positions and interests of the opposing party. Prepare constructive ways to communicate your outcomes and respond to the positions of the other.

Stage 3: Conflict Management

The third stage of the model, conflict management, involves reducing the level of emotional energy (defusing negative emotions) and clarifying and understanding similarities and differences. This allows disputing parties to eliminate or minimize destructive behavior, as well as negative attitudes and feelings toward each other. This settlement may not be an agreement that resolves all the differences, but it may enable the disputing parties to go forward

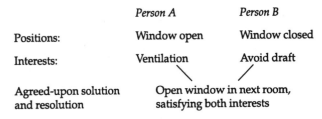

Figure 3.3. Positions versus Interests (Follet, 1940)
Follett, 1940, as cited in Fisher & Ury, 1983.

with an understanding of their differences and mutual respect for one another.

The process involves the parties using reflective listening to change the negative emotional states in the conflict to states that are more amenable to resolving disputes and differences. The process also allows the parties to clarify misunderstandings and facilitate movement from a focus on the past to a focus on the future. Explicit in the process is acknowledging the positive intentions of the other parties, as well as expressing acknowledgment of similarities in points of view.

Should the conflict involve covert issues, probing must be done to determine if projection and transference are involved. If a major covert component seems present, laser listening is required to surface covert issues. This may require increased attention and emotional energy to break down the wall of defenses—such as denial, suppression, and repression—surrounding the covert issue. The main purpose of this step is to prepare the parties to repossess their projected issues. As you attempt to determine the covert issues and face the other party(s) with these issues, you bring them from the undiscussable to discussable. If disowned issues (projections) are surfaced, and the reparation process (reintegration of the disowned issues) takes place, the conflict between the parties may disappear. Should this occur, the likelihood is that the conflict is really a manifestation of an inner conflict of one person. Alternately, even with reparation, there may still be a conflict between the parties, but this conflict is now amenable to determination of overt issues, and reflective listening should be sufficient to manage the conflict.

Whether the conflict is covert or overt, the object of conflict management is to achieve a constructive emotional state in all parties and a clear, mutual understanding of one another's views. If the difference involves beliefs that are intangible (values), success is achieved when there is mutual understanding of similarities and differences and an appreciation of the various points of view. If the differences are tangible (needs), success is achieved when the parties agree to negotiate and arrive at a mutually satisfying solution.

Stage 4: Negotiation

Negotiation, as previously indicated, is a communication process for enabling disputing parties to achieve a mutually agreed-on outcome with respect to their differences. Interest-based negotiation is a particular form of negotiation, the outcome of which is to achieve an integrative agreement. An integrative agreement is one in which all the parties get their interests at least partially satisfied.

Integrative agreements can be thought of in terms of offering joint benefit to the negotiating parties, either in relation to the alternative of not having an agreement or in relation to a compromise. To offer joint benefit, an integrative agreement must provide higher payoffs than a compromise would provide. The formulation of the integrative agreement in terms of the parties' interests can involve a trade-off, or dovetailing, of differences that leads to mutual benefit. This formulation can be the realization of an interest held in common and made into a joint agreement and shared outcome.

Conflict Resolution Process

The process of coping effectively with conflict as it emerges in the moment involves managing the emotion present in the situation and then using a negotiation or problem-solving process to work out a mutually acceptable solution to any differences. Two distinct processes are involved: conflict management and negotiation. Normally in a conflict episode, you will be moving back and forth between managing the emotions to maintain constructive states and negotiating around the differences. These processes illustrated in this chapter are useful in those contexts in which you have physical access to the other party or parties to the conflict. Physical presence is essential to effectively managing emotion and eliciting the constructive emotional states required to actually work out a plan to reduce the differences between the current and desired states of the parties in the conflicts. Applications of these conflict resolution processes are illustrated in Figure 4.1.

Conflict Management

Conflict management is a communication process for creating constructive emotional states in a conflict situation. Constructive

| | | Situations | | | | |
| | | One-on-One | Small Groups (3–20) | Medium Systems (30–100) | Large Systems (Greater than 100) | Between Large Systems |
Context	Process					
Emotion Present	Conflict Management	Yes	Yes	Yes	No	No
Difference Present	Negotiation or Problem Solving	Yes	Yes	Yes	Yes	Yes

Figure 4.1. Applicability of Conflict Resolution Processes

states promote working out a solution to the conflict. Reflective listening is the core skill for conflict management. The process involves listening particularly for the emotion. When emotions are heard, they lessen and become integrated. This reduces the emotional energy and makes room to hear the differences that exist between you and the other parties.

The process differs somewhat between interpersonal conflict and conflict that emerges in a group setting. An eight-step process is used for interpersonal conflict and a six-step process is used for conflict in groups.

Interpersonal Process

The interpersonal process is delineated in Figure 4.2. Each step in the *interpersonal process* for conflict management is described in the following sections.

Step 1. Notice the tension and begin to listen

This step begins when you notice the tension between you and another person. This tension is easily perceived by paying attention to both verbal and physiological cues (facial tension, skin color, tightness around the mouth, set jaw, and so on). You also need to be aware of your own feelings and monitor and control your own emotion.

Changing emotional state

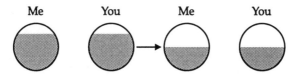

1. Notice the tension and begin to listen—force it at first.
2. Continue listening until you get a YES (means other feels heard).
3. Summarize other's view—getting a YES.
4. State your view.
5. Handle defensiveness.
6. Invite other to summarize your view.
7. Summarize both sides and get a YES.
8. Transition to negotiation. (Diagnose needs vs. beliefs; tangible vs. intangible.)
   • If beliefs—CLOSE (acknowledging similarities and differences)
   • If needs—MOVE TO NEGOTIATION

Figure 4.2. Conflict Management Process—One-to-One

As you become aware of the conflict, begin to reflectively listen, while remembering to pace in order to get and maintain rapport.

Forcing the listening requires discipline. You will want to convince the other of your "rightness," and you'd prefer that he or she would listen to you. *You must take this first step.* It involves giving up lots of airtime. Do some "self-talk" to remind yourself that continued arguing will get you nowhere and that this method will work if you give it a few minutes, though you might not have clear evidence of this in your first few "reflections." Your listening must, overall, show true respect for both the other person and his or her position, even if you are not shown respect in return. Your tone of voice, posture, and facial expression must match the words of your "reflections" in conveying empathy and understanding.

Step 2. Continue to listen—get a "yes"

Reflectively listen until you hear the cue word "yes" (or "exactly" or "that's right"). This "yes" signifies that (a) you really understand the other, and (b) the other really feels understood.

This "yes" is an acknowledgement by the other that he or she is heard. If the other says "yes, but" or continues to talk, you do not yet have a "yes." Sometimes you'll get the "yes" after one "reflection," sometimes not until you've reflected five or six times. On any cycle, it is never your turn to give your opinion until Step 4.

Step 3. Summarize the other's view—get a "yes"

Summarizing involves capturing and stating the essence of the other's view to his or her satisfaction. In this step capture the bottom lines. You do not want to necessarily include all the detail you heard, and you need to get a "yes." It is useful to summarize at a higher logical level or level of abstraction.

Step 4. State your view

Be clear and concise in expressing your view without getting on your "soapbox"; just because you've listened, and you've treated the other with respect, your turn doesn't entitle you to a lengthy monologue. Present your opinion as your opinion without sounding like (or believing) that it's necessarily the only, or even right, opinion. Use your turn to focus on yours and/or the other person's interest. Express why you stand where you do; do not express your position, the particular solution you've concluded. Very few skills help reduce tension more than saying, "It looks like we see the same thing in relation to . . . " and "It seems as if the real difference between us is . . . " Present your side of the issue with clarity.

Step 5. Handle defensiveness

It is to be expected that the other person will react and defend against your view. When this occurs it is critical that you reflectively listen, again making sure you get another "yes."

You may need to summarize your view again, clarifying similarities and differences. Recycle with listening until you get a "yes."

Step 6. Invite summary of your view

Inviting the other to summarize your view seems like an awkward step, and you run the risk of the other saying "no." With rapport and respect, the other will usually attempt to offer you a summary of your position and interests in the conflict.

Usually the other will have misunderstood, and you may need to clarify your view again followed by more reflective listening. You must continue this process until (a) the other hears and can accurately summarize your view to you, (b) you can accurately summarize the other's view, and (c) you have rapport.

Step 7. Summarize both sides—get a "yes"

In this step you summarize both views and get a "yes." You may not have converted the other to your perspective or achieved complete agreement on the content of the conflict.

You will have reduced the emotional energy and managed the conflict. You may still have differences that need to be negotiated, but the highly destructive emotional energy that clouds clear thinking and listening will be gone.

Step 8. Diagnose needs versus beliefs

Following Step 7, the conflict itself, the emotional energy is lessened and you can diagnose the nature of the conflict. If the conflict is intangible, one of belief or around an issue you and the other value differently, you can exit the process at this point, acknowledging the similarities and differences. If the differences are concrete and tangible, it is appropriate to move to a negotiation or problem-solving strategy to arrive at a win/win solution based on both parties' interests.

Group Process

The process for managing conflict in a *group setting* is illustrated in Figure 4.3. Each step in the process is elaborated in the following sections:

Step 1. Notice the tension and say what you see, hear, and feel

Make a statement that is direct, specific, nonjudgmental about your perception of the conflict. Convey a spirit of "There's something we might need to work out . . . " rather than "I'm right and the rest of you are wrong and I need to convince you . . . "

Changing emotional state

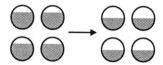

1. Notice the tension and say what you hear, see, and feel.
2. Convey your intentions and the importance of honest interaction.
3. Reflectively listen to
   • individuals
   • themes
   • similarities
   • differences
   • the group as a whole.
4. Summarize positions and interests.
5. Express appreciation.
6. Transition to negotiation. (Diagnose needs vs. beliefs; tangible vs. intangible.)
   • If beliefs—CLOSE (acknowledging similarities and differences)
   • If needs—MOVE TO NEGOTIATION

Figure 4.3. Conflict Mangement Process—Group (as facilitator or group member)

Step 2. Convey the importance to you of honest reaction

Say that you want to hear what they have to tell you, whether or not you're going to like it. The others need to be convinced that you want to hear their opinions, and why, and that they will be safe in telling you the truth.

Step 3. Reflective listening—have the attitude, at all times, of a listener

Begin to reflectively listen, forcing it if necessary. Continue to listen and pace to achieve rapport with all group members.

The listening must be directed five ways:

• To individuals ("What you didn't like, Neil, was that . . . ")
• To similarities ("Sally, you're feeling the same way as Jack . . . ")
• To differences ("You believe X. That's the opposite of Ed's . . . ")

- Themes ("One theme that seems to be emerging is the need for consensus before we proceed . . .")
- To the group as a whole ("So far, it seems like 3 issues. First . . .")

The rationale behind each of these five ways of listening are:

- Individuals: You listen to individuals to make sure each person has a chance to say what he or she feels and to ensure that both you and the person understand what is being said.
- Similarities: You listen to similarities to help you and the group understand the extent of the problem and to provide safety for the speaker by connecting his or her thoughts with others.
- Differences: You listen to differences to prevent dissension within the group, especially if those differing are "adversaries" in a conflict with you. Your integrity here demonstrates that you are interested not only in getting your needs met but in ensuring that the other side gets their needs met as well. This ensures that the conflicting parties stay at peace with each other emotionally. You don't want the conflict management model to create new problems for people. So, when someone shares a position that is contrary to the popular energy being presented, you must protect him or her, while at the same time protecting the person differed with. You do that by listening to the differences.
- Themes: You try to capture recurrent themes or patterns that are emerging from a collection of individuals in the group. These might be in the forms of recurrent thoughts and/or feelings.
- The Group: You listen to the group to make absolutely certain you are totally clear on all the issues raised and to make absolutely certain the group knows you understand their issue(s).

Step 4. Summarize positions and interests—make a clear distinction between this phase and the next

Summarize the specific proposals or stands on the issues (position), as well as the general reasons or motivators (interests) that underlie the proposal or stand on the issues. Following this, capture where the group is in regard to the conflict and the suggested next steps. If a problem needs to be worked out, it is important for the group to know that you know you're not finished yet. The two steps are (a) "Here's where we are, X, Y, Z," and (b) "Here's what we need to do next, A, B, C."

Step 5. Express appreciation

This is a tense, volatile, vulnerable time. If people are willing to go through it with you, and if they are willing to self-disclose honestly, that deserves appreciation. Don't take a smooth process lightly. Everyone is thankful and relieved at the end of a successful intervention, able to breathe a little easier. Acknowledge it!!!

Step 6. Diagnose needs versus beliefs

Following Step 5, the conflict itself, the emotional energy is lessened and you can diagnose the nature of the conflict. If the conflict is intangible, one of belief or around an issue you and the other value differently, you can exit the process at this point, acknowledging the similarities or differences. If the differences are concrete and tangible, it is appropriate to move to a negotiation or problem-solving strategy to arrive at a win/win solution based on both parties' interests.

Negotiation

Negotiation is a communication process for enabling disputing parties to achieve a mutually acceptable solution to their differences. Negotiation processes can be used in the everyday practice of dealing with differences, as well as in the context of a conflict. In the first case, a school administrator can be conversing with a teacher to work on a mutually acceptable schedule for shared decision-making meetings. Differences may emerge and the two use a problem-solving process to explore alternatives and agree on a solution. The process is rational and neither party experiences strong emotion. This is a process of negotiation—creating a joint solution that allows both parties to do better than they might have without the process.

Flexibility is required
to move from negotiation
to conflict and back
in dealing with differences

Figure 4.4. Flexibility Requirements for the Conflict Manager

In the second case, something triggers an emotional exchange between the two, and the negotiation process falters. At this point one of the parties needs to move to conflict management and begin to listen to the other. When the emotional level of both parties returns to normal, the negotiation can proceed. This is an example of conflict management. Often there is a cycling back and forth between conflict management and negotiation in a conflict episode. This requires keen awareness and flexibility on the part of the conflict manager, as indicated in Figure 4.4. In the normal process of dealing with conflict at it emerges, conflict management precedes negotiation.

The essence of negotiation is problem solving. When negotiation is a part of the conflict resolution process, the sequence of steps to be followed involve four key elements: writing a problem statement around the desired state, brainstorming options, evaluating alternatives, and working out an action plan to ensure a well-implemented solution. The process is essentially the same in both interpersonal and group conflicts.

The negotiation process is illustrated in Figure 4.5. The steps are identical for negotiation in both one-on-one and group situations. In both cases the steps are implemented following the conflict management processes illustrated in Figures 4.2 and 4.3.

Each of the steps in the *negotiation process* is described in the following section.

Step 1. Identify and clarify interests

Identifying and clarifying interests is the most critical step in the process. This step involves distinguishing between positions and interests. To do this you first need to identify the initial positions

1. Identify and clarify interests.
2. Develop a problem statement: "How to . . ."
3. Brainstorm options.
4. Evaluate alternatives.
5. Decide on a solution.
6. Develop an action plan.
7. Build in evaluation process.
8. Process experience.

Future Steps
9. Implement the action plan.
10. Evaluate results.

Figure 4.5. Negotiation Process

of all parties. As a skilled person, you need to listen reflectively to each party's position and summarize it to his or her satisfaction. This helps the disputing parties clarify their often initially confused positions. Once the positions are identified, the underlying interests of all parties can be elicited. This involves uncovering the interests of each party that underlie their initial positions—that is, the reasons why the positions are held. You can elicit the interests of the parties to the conflict in a number of ways:

1. "Chunking up" the position to interests. This can be done by asking generalizing questions, such as: "What reasons cause you to hold that position?" "For what reason does that solution appeal to you?" "For what reason does that particular position make sense to you?" "What is important about that position?" "What will that solution give you?"

2. Listening with a "third ear" to the possible meanings that underlie the positions. This involves being attentive to points emphasized and deemphasized, the unique words a person uses, and the specific issues that arouse emotional energy.

3. Intuiting the interests that are likely to underlie positions based on experience.

4. Inferring interests from what the parties have said or how they have behaved in situations external to the conflict situation.

5. Asking others who know the disputants about their beliefs, positions, and what they value.

Interests occur on a hierarchy or range of logical levels: Behind every position is an interest, and behind every interest is a more general interest. A position is a solution at a very low and specific logical level. For instance, a specific position is when a teacher's union demands that class size remains under 25 students for each teacher. The interest that underlies or motivates the specific position (solution) might be "effective classroom instruction." At a higher logical level, the interests might be "so students learn."

This step is concluded by summarizing and gaining agreement on similarities and differences in interests. Focusing on the areas of agreement establishes an "agreement frame," which emphasizes likeness and similarity and increases the probability of rapport between the disputing parties.

Occasionally, at this point, the conflict may be resolved when the parties realize that all the interests can be easily met because enough similarity in interests exists. This can allow the disputing parties to come to speedy agreement around the commonality of their interests and thereby resolve the conflict.

Step 2. Develop a problem statement

Developing a problem statement focuses the parties on the desired state. It incorporates the interests identified in Step 1. Often a separate problem statement is required for each issue in a conflict situation, if there is more than one issue. The format for the problem statement is:

How to   _____   _____.
             (verb)   (desired result)

In this step, test the problem statement and get agreement on it.

Step 3. Brainstorm options

In this step identify and clarify as many options as possible for the solution. Ask the parties to the conflict to suggest possible solutions. Be sure you treat the disputing parties' ideas with respect. Also remember to discourage evaluation until a number of possible options have been proposed. The bottom line in this step is to separate "inventing" from "deciding."

Step 4. Evaluate alternatives

In this step evaluate options for a mutually acceptable solution. In the evaluation process discard options that the parties perceive as "impossible," keeping any that even one person advocates for evaluation. Other possibilities are combining similar options or adding new options to make sure that the options satisfy all parties' interests. A last element in this step is to prioritize the options.

Step 5. Decide on a solution

The ideal solution is one that meets all parties' interests. Often some element of trading interests is involved. Often the solution incorporates a number of the alternatives that can be undertaken in sequence. When a decision appears close, state it so that all parties can understand the solution.

Step 6. Develop an action plan

This step involves the development of an action plan. An action plan is a delineation of the steps to implement the decision, as indicated in Figure 4.6. The action plan specifically sets forth who is to do what, by when. This ensures that the solution agreed to is more likely to be implemented.

Step 7. Build in evaluation process

This step involves developing and building into the action plan a process and step(s) for evaluating the effectiveness of the solution. The evaluation process includes an assessment of the results achieved by the action plan, and it usually involves a conversation during which the parties can express their feelings about what happened or didn't happen. Sometimes replanning is required to repair any failure in the implementation plan.

Step No.	Step Descriptions	Person Responsible	Target Date

Figure 4.6. Action Plan

Step 8. Process experience

This step involves "processing" or talking about the experience of doing the first seven steps together. It is a process of exploring feelings and reactions to the process. In this conversation, you invite the disputing parties to share perspectives on the process and share your own perspectives on the process as well. You can then allow this focus on the process to move the conflict event to a close.

Future steps involve the implementation of the plan and evaluation of results. These steps are labeled Steps 9 and 10 as follows:

Step 9. Implement the action plan

This step involves using the action plan as a guide to the actual resolution of the conflict situation.

Step 10. Evaluate results

This step involves using the evaluation process specified in the action plan to assess the results achieved. This step often involves a concluding conversation to bring the conflict to termination.

Some important points to remember in negotiation, either as an involved party or a third party to the conflict, include:

- Describe the process in one sentence to the parties so they know what will happen.
- Always invite the disputing parties to use the problem-solving method. The parties need to choose the processes they will use.

- Ask permission to take notes and use newsprint (if able) so all can see the development of the process.
- Maintain rapport at all times.
- Reflectively listen to help the disputing parties get their interests stated and met.
- Write down every solution suggested in brainstorming.
- Be open to unusual solutions.
- Don't settle for a solution that doesn't meet at least some of the interests of all parties.
- Respond to your own emotional reactions during the process.
- Be sensitive to the others involved.
- Be congruent and express respect and empathy.

Some suggestions for breaking deadlocks in the negotiation process include:

- Go back to brainstorming to generate additional options.
- Go back to the initial identification of interests and attempt to restate the problem.
- Make a direct appeal to the parties involved—for example: "Can you figure out why we are having trouble finding an acceptable solution? What's blocking us?"
- See whether the parties would be willing to sleep on the problem or reflect on it and resume the process later.
- Ask whether further study or more data would be helpful.
- Call in an outside consultant with content or process expertise.
- Inform the parties of the consequences of failure to come to agreement by a certain time.
- See whether the parties would be willing to try out one of the proposed solutions for a period of time.
- Take a "first step"; leave some areas unresolved for later discussion.

Using problem solving as a negotiation tool is thus an important step in the negotiation and conflict resolution process presented in this chapter.

Conclusion

Conflict is characterized by perceived differences and negative emotional states. The issues in conflict can be thought of as tangible and intangible—as needs or beliefs. Conflict often results in destructive ends, but it doesn't have to be this way. Collaboration and compromise are usually available as alternatives in a conflict situation.

To manage conflict successfully, we propose that the negative emotions that accompany conflict be managed by the strategic use of listening. The differences in needs that underlie conflicts can best be dealt with by interest-based negotiation. By uncovering the interests that underlie the positions of the conflicting parties, solutions that meet those interests can be discovered. The problem-solving process that is embedded in the negotiation process is used to allow the free creation of ideas that will best meet the needs of the parties involved.

Along with becoming aware of conflict situations and preparation steps, we propose a process that incorporates conflict management and negotiation. Using these processes together increases the likelihood that collaborative and acceptable resolutions to conflicts will occur.

Annotated Bibliography and References

Breslin, J. W., & Rubin, J. Z. (1991). *Negotiation theory and practice.* Cambridge, MA: Program in Negotiation.

Forty articles, mainly reprinted from the Harvard Negotiation Journal, written by some of the leading scholar-practitioners in the field. Relevant to negotiation in a wide variety of contexts.

Capelle, R. G. (1979). *Changing human systems.* Toronto: Human Systems Institute.

An interesting and helpful book discussing how human systems function and change along different levels. Includes a chapter on the role of the consultant in the change process.

Condlifee, P. (1991). *Conflict management: A practical guide.* Collingwood, Victoria: Tafe.

A combination "theory-practice" book that provides good review of the literature with skill development and helpful training exercises, role plays, and simulations.

Covey, S. R. (1989). *The seven habits of highly effective people: Powerful lessons in personal change.* New York: Simon & Schuster.

The author describes the requisite knowledge, attitude, and skills for personal and professional effectiveness. Special em-

phasis on the importance of paradigms and principles in developing the character ethic.

Dana, D. (1989). *Managing differences.* Wolcott, CT: MTI.

An easy-to-understand-and-use four-step approach to building better relationships at work and home. Helpful chapter on assessing cost of conflict in your organization.

Fisher, R., & Ury, W. (1983). *Getting to Yes: Negotiating Agreement Without Giving In.* New York: Penguin.

A vastly popular book that has widely influenced the theory and practice of the negotiation field. A hands-on, practical small book with numerous helpful examples.

Hocker, J. L., & Wilmot, W. W. (1991). *Interpersonal conflict* (3rd ed.). Dubuque, IA: Wm. C. Brown.

A good blend of applied theory and practical exercises covering such topics as power, tactics and styles, assessment, and third party intervention.

Kahn, S. D. (1988). *Peacemaking: A systems approach to conflict management.* Lanham, MD: University Press of America.

A fascinating book by a consulting psychologist that incorporates insights from quantum physics, system theory, Jungian psychology, and Tavistock group theory to explore problem solving and peacemaking at the interpersonal and group level.

Katz, N. H., & Lawyer, J. W. (1983, Fall). Communication and conflict management skills: Strategies for individual and systems change. *National Forum, 63*(4).

The authors use an intervention in a large school system to describe their intervention decisions and philosophy, as well as their training approach in communication and conflict management skills.

Katz, N. H., & Lawyer, J. W. (1985). *Communication and Conflict Resolution Skills.* Dubuque, IA: Kendall/Hunt.

A self-instructive, highly readable workbook with a variety of examples and exercises on listening, problem solving, assertion, and negotiation.

Kriesberg, L. (1982). *Social conflicts* (2nd ed.). Englewood Cliffs, NJ: Prentice Hall.

*A widely quoted and foundational book on social conflict theory
that is critical to understanding the variations, stages, and possible consequences of social conflict.*

Laborde, G. Z. (1988). *Influencing with integrity: Management skills
for communication and negotiation.* Palo Alto, CA: Syntony.

*A lively and provocative book that incorporates insights from
neurolinguistic programming to enhance the practice of ad-
vanced communication and negotiation. Very helpful chapter
on making meetings work.*

Pruitt, D. G., & Rubin J. Z. (1986). *Social conflict: Escalation, stale-
mate, and settlement.* New York: Random House.

*One of the classic books in describing major factors that lead to
escalation and de-escalation of conflict. Critical concepts dis-
cussed include integrative solutions and a variety of third-
party intervention roles.*

Ury, W. (1991). *Getting past no: Negotiating your way from confrontation to cooperation,* New York: Bantam.

*A practical guide to dealing with "difficult people." A five-step
approach for turning tough, stubborn adversaries into negotiating partners.*

Weeks, D. (1992). *The eight essential steps to conflict resolution.* Los
Angeles: Tarcher.

*An easy-to-follow, step-by-step approach to the theory and
practice of "conflict partnership."*